The Art of
Animation

The Art of
Animation

Craig E. Blohm and Hal Marcovitz

ReferencePoint
Press®

San Diego, CA

© 2020 ReferencePoint Press, Inc.
Printed in the United States

For more information, contact:
ReferencePoint Press, Inc.
PO Box 27779
San Diego, CA 92198
www.ReferencePointPress.com

LIBRARY OF CONGRESS CATALOGING-IN-PUBLICATION DATA

Names: Blohm, Craig E., 1948– author. | Marcovitz, Hal, author.
Title: The Art of Animation/by Craig E. Blohm and Hal Marcovitz.
Description: San Diego, CA: ReferencePoint Press, Inc., 2020. | Series: Art Scene | Includes bibliographical references and index. | Audience: Grades 9 to 12.
Identifiers: LCCN 2019018552 (print) | LCCN 2019018719 (ebook) | ISBN 9781682825785 (eBook) | ISBN 9781682825778 (hardback)
Subjects: LCSH: Animated films—Juvenile literature. | Animated television programs—Juvenile literature.
Classification: LCC NC1765 (ebook) | LCC NC1765 .B59 2020 (print) | DDC 791.43/34—dc23
LC record available at https://lccn.loc.gov/2019018552

$\mathcal{C}$ONTENTS

Introduction

Animation Transformation

It happened nearly every Saturday morning in homes across America. While parents enjoyed the luxury of getting a few extra hours of sleep, their children padded to the kitchen, poured a bowl of sugary cereal, and plopped down on the living room couch to enjoy a morning of animated entertainment. In the prosperous post–World War II era of the 1950s and 1960s, the new medium of television brought visual entertainment into the home for the first time. Popular prime-time evening shows generally included sitcoms, westerns, medical dramas, and variety shows. But Saturday mornings and after school on weekdays belonged mostly to animated cartoons produced for a young audience.

Kids had a wealth of cartoons to entertain them. Animated characters such as Bugs Bunny, Daffy Duck, and Woody Woodpecker had gotten their start in theaters during the 1940s and 1950s. Kiddie matinees offered hours of popcorn, kid-friendly movies, and cartoons each Saturday afternoon. Whether shown in theaters or on television, animated cartoons were usually viewed as entertainment for children only, undeserving of the attention of adults.

Cartoons Grow Up

As television and its audience grew more sophisticated, so did cartoons. By the 1960s, some cartoons began incorporating humor that only adults would recognize while keeping the slapstick that children enjoyed. For example, the 1960s fell within an era of great international tension between America and the Soviet Union known as the Cold War. It was a conflict waged largely behind the scenes as diplomats and spies attempted to gain the upper hand for one country or the other. But adult viewers of the animated show *The Adventures of Rocky and Bullwinkle* found reasons to laugh at the Cold War. The stars of the show—a plucky squirrel named Rocky and his pal, the dim-witted moose Bullwinkle—often found themselves looking for ways to outwit the dastardly (yet humorous) plans of Cold War–era spies Boris and Natasha. Author Keith Scott comments,

> "[*The Adventures of Rocky and Bullwinkle*] was the first show in the history of TV animation to blatantly—healthily—thumb its nose at the establishment. In today's parlance, it had 'attitude.'"[1]
>
> —Writer Keith Scott

It's often been noted that in tough times, those in need of an escape turn to the release offered by comedy for a welcome wry laugh at shared misfortune. In particular, comedy with an edge, containing jokes that don't just play safe but tell a few home truths. The moose and squirrel strike that chord. . . . The cartoons overflow with great jokes and puncturing satire. It was the first show in the history of TV animation to blatantly—healthily—thumb its nose at the establishment. In today's parlance, it had "attitude."[1]

Still, if parents wanted to watch the antics of Rocky and Bullwinkle, they had to join their children on Saturday mornings in front of the TV. Soon, though, animated series would be aired in the evenings. In 1960 the animated show *The Flintstones* debuted in so-called prime time. *The Flinstones*, which recounted the antics of a family living during the Stone Age, took its premise from *The Honeymooners*, an earlier live-action comedy program about an oafish, bumbling husband and his ever-patient wife. *The Jetsons*, a cartoon about a family living in the future, where robots were employed as housekeepers and fathers zoomed to work in hovercrafts, made its prime-time debut in 1962. Both shows portrayed life from an adult perspective, with themes of family relations, working, and getting along with the boss and the neighbors. But they still featured plenty of comedy for the kids.

Like live-action sitcoms of the era, *The Flintstones* and *The Jetsons* portrayed an idealized version of life: parents were loving, kids were mischievous but good, and problems were solved in thirty minutes. During the late 1980s, however, all that was about to change.

Meet the Simpsons

In 1989 a new type of family came to prime time. *The Simpsons*, the brainchild of cartoonist Matt Groening, portrayed perhaps the most dysfunctional family on TV. The father, Homer, is a lazy, beer- and donut-loving blue-collar worker; his wife, Marge, is a helpful but usually ineffective mom. The Simpson kids—Maggie, Lisa, and especially bad-boy Bart—try their parents' patience at every turn. It is an exaggerated but all too real look at the modern family at its worst.

And yet it entertains both young people and adults. As journalist Joe Morgenstern explains, "Young viewers love the show's exuberant humor. . . . Grown-ups relish its broad gags, just as the kids do, but also respond to its emotional complexity and its wickedly deadpan social comments."[2] Such emotional complexity, made integral to the cartoon, has changed the animated landscape forever. Other prime-time animated shows began pushing the boundaries of adult themes, among them *King of the Hill*, *Family Guy*, and *South Park*, giving adults new reasons to tune in to a medium that began as innocuous children's entertainment.

In addition to creating animated works that revolve around more adult themes, today's animators are experimenting with

> "Young viewers love [*The Simpsons*'] exuberant humor. . . . Grown-ups relish its broad gags, just as the kids do, but also respond to its emotional complexity and its wickedly deadpan social comments."[2]
>
> —Journalist Joe Morgenstern

The Simpsons *affectionately depicts a dysfunctional American family. The show's distinctive characters, exuberant humor, emotional complexity, and social commentary pushed the boundaries of traditional animation.*

new techniques (or in some cases reviving older ones) and seeking out new venues for connecting with fans. No longer limited to movie theaters, network TV, or cable stations, animation is now widely available on Internet-streaming services such as Amazon Prime and Netflix. These and other venues provide artists more options to reach fans and viewers more options to watch their favorite animated series. Viewers can, for example, watch an entire season of the Netflix adventure series *Trollhunters* in one sitting, if they desire. And as animation moves into the future, the line between live-action movies and animated films may become increasingly blurred, as animators make use of sophisticated computer software to make their characters come alive.

CHAPTER ONE

The History of Animation

For millennia, artists have created works that represent the world as they see it through painting, drawing, sculpture, and photography. Due to the nature of these media, things that moved could only be portrayed as static objects. A painting of a flight of birds or a sculpture of a galloping horse could depict the motion of these creatures, but only by capturing them frozen in a single moment in time. Although these early artists may have wished for a way to show motion in their works, such progress would have to wait for the right technology to be developed.

In 1825 British physician John Ayrton Paris invented a device called a thaumatrope, which consisted of a disk with a different picture on each side. When the thaumatrope was rapidly spun by attached strings, the two images could be seen at the same time. Still, such early devices as the thaumatrope were far too simple to tell stories that audiences could find endearing. Indeed, animation as a popular form of art could not take a large step forward until the film industry itself found the technology that enabled movies to be produced and showcased to audiences.

By the late nineteenth century, inventors had perfected cameras capable of filming motion as well as projectors that could present the movies in theaters. With more and more people enjoying motion pictures, filmmakers looked for new ways to entertain them. Filmmaker James Stuart Blackton noticed that odd things sometimes occurred when his camera was stopped and started: objects appeared to move by themselves or pop in and out of the scene. In 1906 Blackton used this as a creative tool for a short

Pictured is a frame from the 1906 animated film Humorous Phases of Funny Faces. *In this film, characters on a blackboard appeared to draw themselves and react to each other.*

film titled *Humorous Phases of Funny Faces*, in which characters on a blackboard appeared to draw themselves and react to each other. The illusion was created by stopping and starting the camera, a technique known as stop-motion animation.

Gertie and Bobby Bumps

Humorous Phases of Funny Faces displayed a crude form of early animation, but before long more sophisticated animated films began to appear. In 1914 cartoonist Winsor McCay introduced an animated dinosaur into a stage act with a film he called *Gertie the Dinosaur*. McCay interacted onstage with Gertie, who appeared to obey his commands. Audiences were enthralled by McCay's animated beast, whose creation became a milestone of animation. Author Stephen Cavalier says *Gertie the Dinosaur* "is often regarded as the first instance of true character animation in the sense that, for the first time, an animated creation had a distinct personality of its own."[3] To animate Gertie, McCay and his assistants rendered the character onto some four thousand sheets of rice paper and then mounted the paper drawings onto sheets of cardboard. He then used a rotary device to quickly flip the cardboard sheets, using a film camera to record the motions of the images.

A year after McCay produced *Gertie the Dinosaur*, another animator took the process a step further—introducing a technical advancement that would dominate the craft of animation for the next century. In 1915 animator Earl Hurd produced a cartoon series featuring a character named Bobby Bumps, drawing the images on celluloid sheets—a process known in the industry as cel animation. Animators found that the translucent sheets had many advantages over paper images. For starters, instead of having to redraw each frame separately, the backgrounds could be drawn on paper and then used over and over again behind the translucent cels, which featured the characters and their movements. As J.P. Telotte, a professor of film and media studies at Georgia Tech University, explains,

"This technique . . . increased efficiency, since only the image produced on each cel would have to be redrawn for every element of a character's motion."[4]

—J.P. Telotte, a professor of film and media studies at Georgia Tech University

This technique not only increased efficiency, since only the image produced on each cel would have to be redrawn for every element of a character's motion, but also produced an effective visual separation of characters and backgrounds. And those effects would only be enhanced by adding other cels, which made it possible to do multiple layers of animation, thereby suggesting a more complex, indeed more natural, world. The effect of that approach shows up repeatedly in the composition of many of his Bobby Bumps efforts.[4]

Early Animation Devices

Long before the invention of movie cameras and projectors, inventors sought ways to produce animation that could be viewed by audiences. In 1832 a device called the phenakistoscope was invented by Belgian physicist Joseph Plateau. The device takes its name from Greek words meaning "to deceive the eye." It was a large paper disk containing numerous slits cut into its edge.

Below the slits were pictures that displayed an action drawn sequentially. The drawings might be of a couple dancing, for example, and each picture differed slightly from the previous one. By spinning the phenakistoscope and looking through the slits at a mirror, the viewer could see the reflected pictures appear to move in a continuous, animated sequence. Film historian Richard J. Leskosky comments that "the phenakistoscope holds special significance as the first device to produce an illusion of motion which we might term 'full animation' in some meaningful sense."

In 1834 British mathematician William George Horner invented a device he called the daedalum, or "wheel of the devil." It improved on the phenakistoscope by enabling more than one person to view a scene at the same time. The daedalum did not become popular until more than thirty years later, when American inventor William F. Lincoln patented the device and gave it an improved name, the zoetrope, meaning "wheel of life."

Richard J. Leskosky, "Phenakistoscope: 19th Century Science Turned to Animation," *Film History*, 1993, pp. 176–89. www.jstor.org.

The Golden Age of Animation

By the late 1920s, cel animation had become the dominant form of the art at Hollywood's animation studios, including a studio run by Walt Disney. But in 1928, Disney's studio was teetering on collapse because a man who distributed films featuring the studio's most popular character, a rabbit named Oswald, had stolen away not only Oswald but most of the animators who drew him. Not one to give up, Disney and his remaining animator, Ub Iwerks, came up with a new character: a mouse named Mickey who had big round ears, two-button shorts, and a mischievous spirit.

Bugs Bunny, the wise-cracking cartoon character, helped propel Warner Bros. (now known as WB) to animation heights. This took place during a period that has been described as animation's golden age.

At a time when sound was just becoming a part of movies, Disney made the bold decision to add sound to his third Mickey Mouse film, a six-minute cartoon called *Steamboat Willie*. Released in November 1928, the film was an immediate success. Audiences and critics raved about the antics of Mickey as a steamboat captain, with music and sound effects perfectly synchronized with the on-screen action. The *New York Times* called *Steamboat Willie* "an ingenious piece of work with a good deal of fun. It growls, whines, squeaks and makes various other sounds that add to its mirthful quality."[5]

Disney expanded his roster of lovable characters, adding animated adventures featuring Donald Duck, Goofy, and Pluto, among others. As Disney cartoons drew audiences into theaters, other studios were prompted to invest in animation and introduce new characters. Warner Bros. (WB) produced two series of cartoons under the names *Looney Tunes* and *Merrie Melodies* featuring such characters as Daffy Duck, Elmer Fudd, Porky Pig, Sylvester and Tweety, and many more. WB soon surpassed Disney as the most successful cartoon producer, largely due to the studio's wise-cracking animated star, Bugs Bunny. Other unforgettable characters of the era were Woody Woodpecker from the Walter Lantz Studio, Terrytoons' Mighty Mouse, and the spinach-loving sailor Popeye from the Max Fleischer Studio.

The popularity of these cartoons during this era has prompted film historians to label it the golden age of animation. Certainly, new technologies introduced into animation art during this era played a role in making cartoons extremely popular. For example, after incorporating sound into his cartoons, Disney began experimenting with color. The studio's 1932 *Flowers and Trees*, animated in full color, became a hit. It was the first animated short to win an Academy Award, the film industry's top prize. Other studios soon added color as well.

Full-Length Movies

With the addition of color, the artistry also improved. Crudely drawn characters with rubbery arms and legs that could stretch to fantastic proportions were replaced by more multidimensional characters whose looks and actions seemed somehow more believable. Chuck Jones, who animated Bugs Bunny and later created the *Road Runner* cartoon series, recalled, "A small child once said to me: 'You don't draw Bugs Bunny, you draw pictures of Bugs Bunny.' That's a very profound observation because it means he thinks that the characters are alive, which, as far as I'm concerned, is true. And, I feel the same way about animation. . . . Animation isn't an illusion of life. It is life."[6]

> "A small child once said to me: 'You don't draw Bugs Bunny, you draw pictures of Bugs Bunny.'"[6]
>
> —Animator Chuck Jones

The Very Limited Animation of *Clutch Cargo*

Budget restrictions prevented early TV animators from employing the type of artistic animation audiences were used to seeing in movie theaters. To save money, TV animators of the 1950s and 1960s resorted to limited animation, in which just a few elements of the characters' bodies were animated. Perhaps no cartoon series of the era animated its characters less than *Clutch Cargo*.

The title character was a globe-trotting pilot who faced danger in every episode, accompanied by a young sidekick named Spinner and his dog, Paddlefoot. Other than the characters' lips, though, very little else in the show was animated. The animators produced the show by filming the moving lips of the voice actors reading their scripts, then superimposing the lips onto mostly still drawings depicting the action. The process of projecting the live lips onto the inked cels was developed by Edwin Gillette, a TV camera operator, who named the process Synchro-Vox. According to Emil Sitka, an actor who voiced the dialogue for several characters on the show, "If you think those cartoons look strange, it was even stranger to work on them. First, they'd put makeup around my mouth and put this kind of garish lipstick on my lips. Then they'd strap me down in a chair and brace my head."

Clutch Cargo debuted in 1959. It was syndicated to local TV stations throughout America but was canceled in 1960.

Quoted in MeTV, "8 Lip-Smacking Facts About *Clutch Cargo*," 2019. www.metv.com.

While Bugs Bunny and Mickey Mouse were entertaining young and old in six- to seven-minute animated shorts, studios were expanding their on-screen horizons with feature-length animated films. Disney was first to release a movie-length animated feature in 1937 when the studio produced *Snow White and the Seven Dwarfs*. Produced at a cost of nearly $1.5 million, *Snow White* delighted moviegoers with its catchy tunes, the animated antics of seven jovial dwarfs, a crafty villain, a beautiful heroine, and a dashing prince. Animators modeled their drawings on the movements of live actors, which added a note of realism to the fairy tale. After the success of *Snow White and the Seven Dwarfs*, Disney went on to create more features, including *Pinocchio*, *Dumbo*, and *Bambi*.

Cartoons and Television

Although animated films such as *Snow White and the Seven Dwarfs* and *Bambi* were visually stunning, it was not the type of animation that would come to dominate the 1950s. By then, the new medium of television brought entertainment right into America's living rooms; by 1954 more than half of all American homes had a TV set. Attendance at theaters declined as people preferred to stay home and watch free programs—including cartoons—on television rather than pay for a show at the local movie theater.

Cartoons may have found a new home in television, but the small screen was quite different from the big theaters. One of the biggest differences was money: The fledgling medium of TV had little cash to create cartoons for its audience. Animation was expensive and time-consuming to produce, so animation studios had to come up with production shortcuts. Full animation in the traditional style was replaced by limited animation in which only certain portions of a frame are redrawn. For example, when a character talked, only the mouth would move while the rest of the body remained still. Or when the character walked, the arms did not swing and the head did not turn; only the legs would move. Although less realistic and artistic than traditional cartoons, television viewers—especially the target audience of children—did not seem to mind.

Animating by Computer

Though the artistic qualities of animation may have stalled for a time, a growing technology behind the scenes soon pushed animation in new directions. By the 1970s computers were being used in accounting, journalism, sales, and many other fields. Computers also found their way into animation. Indeed, the computer enabled artists to bring a whole new level of animation to the screen. Animation had always been time- and labor-intensive, but the computer gave animators a new tool to make their job easier, faster, and, in some instances, even more creative.

Computers first had an impact on the cel animation process. At the standard film speed of twenty-four frames for each second of screen time, it takes thousands of cels to create a few minutes of animation. This process was greatly accelerated by using computers to color the individual cels, saving time and money. Disney's Computer Animation Production System (CAPS) could color cels using newly available shading and blending techniques as well as combine cels with backgrounds and perform complicated camera movements within the computer. The 1990 film *Rescuers Down Under* was the first animated film produced using CAPS technology.

Computer-Generated Imagery

As computers grew more powerful, it became clear that animated films could be produced entirely within the computer system, without any physical cels or background paintings. The process is known as computer-generated imagery (CGI). This meant that the art for the characters, backgrounds, and other elements of a film were no longer created by artists working on celluloid sheets but rather by artists working on computer screens. Through newly developed software programs, animators were not only able to create the art on the computer but also to use the computer to fully animate the characters.

The first films to employ CGI were not animated movies but rather live-action films—mostly in the science fiction and horror genres. In the past, to produce special effects for such movies, filmmakers may have had to employ techniques that often failed to convince audiences that what they were seeing was real. For example, the 1931 movie *Dracula*—regarded as a classic in the horror film genre—told the story of a Hungarian count with the power to change into a blood-sucking vampire bat. In one scene, the bat flies in through the bedroom window of a victim. But to show the bat fluttering in through the window, the filmmakers were forced to suspend a puppet bat on strings—a visual effect that is obvious to audiences. Similarly, in 1954 the original *Godzilla* film features a giant reptile stomping through downtown Tokyo—but arguably few people in the audience were fooled into thinking the monster was anything more than an actor wearing a costume.

But CGI is able to help convince people that what they are seeing is—if not real—at least believable. The 1977 film *Star Wars*—the first episode in the highly successful series that is still producing prequels and sequels for contemporary audiences—was one of the first films to use CGI. A pivotal scene near the conclusion of the film, as hero Luke Skywalker navigates his fighter across the mechanical terrain of the Death Star, was filmed using CGI. In the film, the terrain speeds by under Skywalker's fighter as he heads for an exhaust port to drop a torpedo into the enemy vessel. It took computer animators a month to produce two minutes of this action. Ultimately, director George Lucas cut the animation down to a mere forty seconds for the film's final cut. But the action is riveting, and audiences cheered as Skywalker approached the exhaust port, triggered the torpedo, and crippled the evil Empire.

Characters Viewers Could Love

CGI soon found its way into fully animated features. In 1984 Disney produced the cel-animated film *The Little Mermaid*, but the final scene of the film—which depicts the wedding of Ariel and Prince Eric—was produced through CGI. And in 1991, another Disney animated movie, *Beauty and the Beast*, featured scenes produced through CGI. Most of the film is cel animated, but the backgrounds in the ballroom sequence, in which Belle first dances with the Beast, were rendered through CGI. By employing CGI, the animators were able to add a three-dimensional perspective to the scene. Indeed, as the dance sequence unfolds, audiences continually see the characters' viewpoints as they spin through the action. According to Jim

Hillin, who served as supervisor of CGI effects for *Beauty and the Beast*,

> The ballroom sequence features the first computer-generated color background to be both animated and fully dimensional. What this means is that the background is literally moving and the [cel] animators had to animate to it. . . . This gives the advantage of sweeping camera moves and perspectives as well as theatrical lighting that would otherwise be impossible. It introduces live action techniques into the animated world. Here the camera plays a very important role in establishing the mood and helps us to experience what the characters themselves are feeling.[7]

The background in the ballroom sequence of the 1991 animated film Beauty and the Beast *was rendered through CGI. With CGI, the animators were able to give a three-dimensional perspective to the scene.*

In 1995 *Toy Story* became the first animated film produced completely through CGI, enthralling both audiences and critics. Cowboy Woody, astronaut Buzz Lightyear, and others appear on the screen as fully rounded, three-dimensional characters. And although the stars of the film are toys, the story and animation made them characters that viewers could love. "*Toy Story* is a treasure that ushered in another golden age of animation," writes film critic Josh Larsen. "When Woody . . . perks up in the opening scene, it's not only the toy cowboy who comes alive—we're watching the rebirth of an art form."[8] The success of *Toy Story* and numerous other animated films created through CGI, such as *The Incredibles*, *Shrek*, and *Despicable Me*, illustrate how the art of animation has reached new heights since the pioneering work of Winsor McCay, Earl Hurd, and Walt Disney. Today animation is a multibillion-dollar industry featuring electrifying new developments that continually push the art in new and exciting directions.

CHAPTER TWO

Artists of Influence

The art of animation has enthralled audiences for decades, providing fantastic stories that are constrained only by the limits of the animators' imaginations. Luckily for fans, the professionals who work in animation would seem to have limitless creativity. Their stories have taken audiences back into mythical times as well as far into the future as they envision life on other planets. Among the professionals who have shaped the art of animation are John Lasseter, a pioneer in CGI; Nora Twomey, whose work in cel animation has helped call attention to the plight of oppressed women in Afghanistan; Miguel Jiron, whose work on *Spider-Man: Into the Spider-Verse* has brought the art of the comic book to CGI; and Niki Lindroth von Bahr, whose films have helped keep alive the century-old technique known as stop-motion animation.

John Lasseter: Bringing Toys to Life

If Walt Disney could have peered into the future, he might have seen himself reflected in the round, bespectacled face of John Lasseter. As with most kids growing up during the 1960s, Lasseter spent hours watching cartoons on TV. His mother, a high school art teacher, encouraged his growing interest in animation, providing him with paper and crayons. After seeing the Disney animated feature *The Sword in*

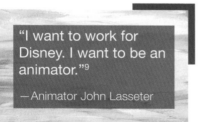

"I want to work for Disney. I want to be an animator."[9]

—Animator John Lasseter

the Stone, he decided on his career, telling his mother, "I want to work for Disney. I want to be an animator."[9]

Lasseter learned the techniques of animation at the California Institute of the Arts, known as CalArts, where two of his short animated films won Student Academy Awards. After Lasseter

Toy Story *was the world's first feature-length computer-animated film. Its creators, John Lasseter and Pixar, used their talents to create characters that were completely believable and likable.*

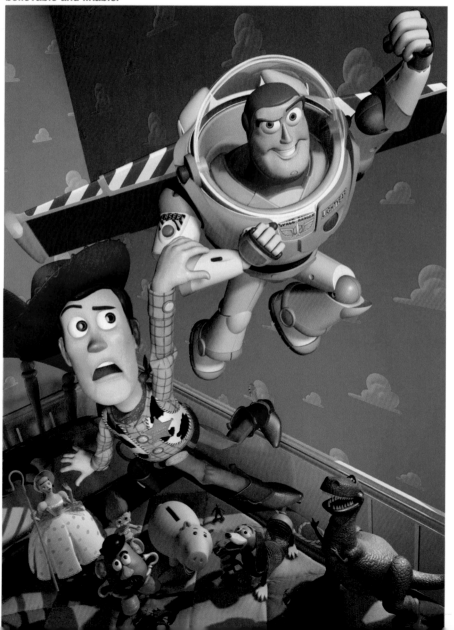

graduated in 1979, Disney hired him as an animator. But working at Disney soon became creatively stifling, as the older animators snubbed Lasseter's ideas. Lasseter had begun to experiment with animation by computer, but his bosses considered the technique too expensive. He was ultimately fired.

Lasseter was not jobless for long. He was soon hired to be part of the computer division of Lucasfilm, a production compa-

Stop-Motion Master Ray Harryhausen

One of the most riveting moments in the 1963 sword-and-sorcery film *Jason and the Argonauts* occurs near the end of the movie, when seven human skeletons emerge from the ground and, armed with swords, launch an attack on the three Greek heroes seeking the mythical Golden Fleece. The scene was filmed using stop-motion animation by veteran Hollywood animator Ray Harryhausen. Recalling the tedious process employed to produce the human-skeleton sword fight, Harryhausen said,

> Each of the model skeletons was about 8 to 10 inches [20 to 25 cm] high. . . . When all the skeletons have manifested themselves to Jason and his men, they are commanded . . . to "Kill, kill, kill them all," and we hear an unearthly scream. What follows is a sequence of which I am very proud. I had three men fighting seven skeletons, and each skeleton had five appendages to move in each separate frame of film. This meant at least 35 animation movements, each synchronized to the actors' movements. Some days I was producing less than one second of screen time; in the end the whole sequence took a record four and a half months.

Harryhausen provided stop-motion effects for seventeen films between the 1940s and the 1980s. Born in 1920, he studied art and animation at the University of Southern California. Before his death in 2013, Harryhausen and his wife established the Ray and Diana Harryhausen Foundation to preserve the hundreds of models he crafted for stop-motion Hollywood films and to provide scholarships for student stop-motion animators.

Ray Harryhausen and Tony Dalton, *Ray Harryhausen: An Animated Life*. New York: Billboard, 2004, p. 170.

ny established by director George Lucas. Working with the early graphics computers that Lucasfilm was developing, Lasseter made *The Adventures of André and Wally B.*, the first animated short that used computers to create both background and characters. In 1986 the computer division became an independent company named Pixar. That same year, Lasseter created the first computer-animated film under the Pixar name, *Luxo, Jr.* Although the film's characters were two desk lamps, the result was a surprisingly charming vignette that audiences enjoyed. Lasseter says, "In that short little film, computer animation went from a novelty to a serious tool for filmmaking."[10]

In 1991 Disney made a deal with Pixar to produce three feature-length films, all to be animated using Pixar's computer-animation system. The first of the films was *Toy Story*, featuring a little boy's toys that come to life. *Toy Story* would become the first feature-length computer-animated film, a daunting task for fledgling Pixar. As cowriter and director, Lasseter made sure that the film was character driven, as in *Luxo, Jr.*, and that the characters were believable and likable. That he succeeded is evident in the box office triumph of *Toy Story* and its influence on the way animated films would be made from then on. Lasseter went on to produce or direct three *Toy Story* sequels as well as *Finding Nemo*, *Cars*, *The Incredibles*, *Frozen*, and other animated hits.

Nora Twomey and the Cartoon Saloon

Born in Cork City, Ireland, Nora Twomey was an indifferent student in primary school during the 1980s, but art captured her interest. "As I continued on at school," Twomey remembers, "and really didn't fit into the mold of school, I retreated more and more into my imagination and more into drawing. My copybooks, the backs of them, were full of doodles. For me, I suppose, it became a stronger, as opposed to a weaker, thing."[11] After struggling in secondary school, Twomey dropped out at the age of fifteen, unsure of what she really wanted to do. She ultimately took a job

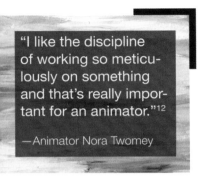
working for a local craftsperson, where her interest in art was rekindled. Twomey entered Ballyfermot College of Further Education in Dublin, where she studied animation. "As soon as I started there," she recalls, "I realized this was perfect for me. I like the discipline of working so meticulously on something and that's really important for an animator."[12]

In 1999, four years after graduating from Ballyfermot, Twomey teamed up with two other graduates of the college, Tomm Moore and Paul Young, to form the animation studio Cartoon Saloon. Two of the studio's feature films, *The Secret of Kells* and *Song of the Sea* were nominated for Academy Awards for Best Animated Feature Film in 2010 and 2015, respectively. Twomey had been the voice director on *The Secret of Kells* and the codirector for *Song of the Sea*. Now she was ready to direct her first animated feature film.

The story for Twomey's directorial debut is taken from the young adult book *The Breadwinner* by writer Deborah Ellis. It is the story of Parvana, an eleven-year-old girl living in Afghanistan under the repressive rule of the fundamentalist Islamic regime known as the Taliban. When her father is arrested, leaving the family without income, Parvana disguises herself as a boy to be able to purchase food for the family as well as search for her father. To help transform the book into an animated feature-length film, Twomey reached out to actress and human rights activist Angelina Jolie, who has lobbied for women's rights in Afghanistan. Jolie's input lent authenticity to the film, advising Twomey not only on the script and voices but on Afghanistan's culture as well.

As director, Twomey was the guiding hand for more than one hundred animators working for Cartoon Saloon. In order to infuse the film with realism, she acted out each scene so that animators could translate real-life movements to characters created on the computer. The film's look runs the gamut from the gritty streets of Kabul to colorful scenes of a fantasy world that Parvana turns into a story to soothe her younger brother.

The Breadwinner premiered in 2017 to critical acclaim, becoming the third out of three feature-length films from Cartoon

Nora Twomey cofounded the animation studio Cartoon Saloon. As director of The Breadwinner, which debuted in 2017 to critical acclaim, Twomey guided dozens of animators who infused the film with a remarkable sense of realism.

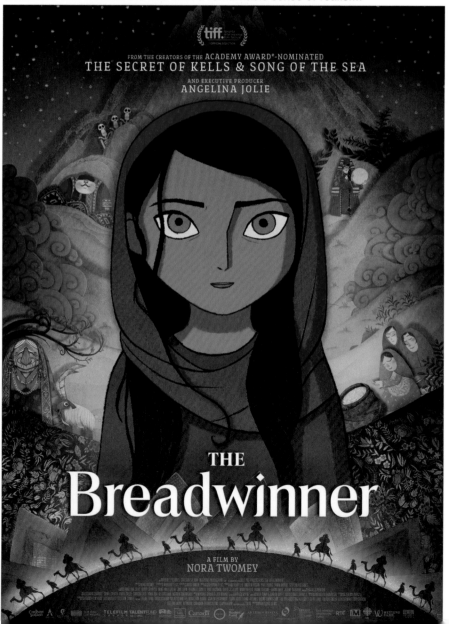

Saloon to be nominated for Academy Awards. Although it did not win, *The Breadwinner* has a story to tell about how the Afghan people have been affected by war. Twomey explains:

> There's a massive Afghan diaspora across the globe now from the generations of conflict that have happened there, and there has been huge regeneration in Afghanistan as well. It's interesting having made this film and meeting so many Afghan people at different screenings—Afghan designers, musicians, artists. Just seeing that really take hold again in the country is really inspirational and a very positive thing to see as well.[13]

Miguel Jiron: Into the Spider-Verse

The 2018 film *Spider-Man: Into the Spider-Verse* broke new ground in CGI, but not because the film showcased new, cutting-edge technologies. Rather, critics and audiences were captivated with the film for the simple reason that the animators elected to dial back the CGI, making it appear as though the characters were still populating the pages of a Marvel comic book—the venue where Spider-Man made his debut back in 1962. According to Miguel Jiron, one of the film's chief animators, "A lot of it is embracing the same foundational elements of traditional animation which is hand drawing—just instead of paper, we're doing it on computers. . . . So basically, embracing what was great about traditional animation techniques while embracing modern technology and tools to help—that was kind of the sweet spot."[14]

Jiron served as the storyboard artist for *Spider-Man: Into the Spider-Verse*, sketching each scene of the film as he followed the script. Essentially, he conceived the look of the movie. The computer animators then followed his sketches, bringing his vision to life. It was a significant role for Jiron, who grew up in Baton Rouge, Louisiana, and turned to art as a young boy during the 1990s as a fan of TV cartoons as well as Disney animated films.

America's Top Animation School

John Lasseter studied animation at the California Institute of the Arts, known as CalArts, in Santa Clarita, California. Lasseter is one of many graduates of the program to go on to careers in animation. The school was founded by brothers Walt and Roy Disney in 1961 when they purchased two small art colleges and merged them into a single university. In 1970, a new campus opened, featuring an extensive program in animation.

Among the graduates of the CalArts animation program is Tim Burton, a well-known director of animated features, including *Frankenweenie*, released in 2012, and *Corpse Bride*, released in 2005. As he was preparing to leave high school, Burton recalls, "I never saw myself going to a real school—I wasn't that great of a student." But he found himself at home at CalArts. "You know, you usually kind of feel alone in that way, like you're the outcast in your school," says Burton. "And then all of a sudden you go to this school filled with outcasts! I think the rest of CalArts thought the . . . animation people were the geeks and weirdos. It was the first time you met people that you could kind of relate to, in a strange way."

CalArts is annually ranked by experts as the nation's top animation school. The website Animation Career Review writes, "Crowned the 'Harvard Business School of Animation' by the *Los Angeles Times*, CalArts has produced hundreds of successful alumni who have generated billions at the box office worldwide."

Quoted in Sam Kashner, "The Class That Roared," *Vanity Fair*, March 2014. www.vanityfair.com.

Animation Career Review, "Top 50 Animation Schools and Colleges in the US—2019 College Rankings," February 22, 2019. www.animationcareerreview.com.

He says, "I drew compulsively throughout my childhood. . . . As I grew older, I became more interested in filmmaking and contemporary art, but at some point, I wanted to make my drawings move and tell stories."[15]

After high school, Jiron learned the art of animation at the University of Southern California (USC), where he received a master's degree in fine arts in 2013 from USC's cinematic arts program. After graduation, he joined the Illumination Entertainment animation studio, where he was assigned to help produce the animation for the studio's 2016 CGI-animated feature *The Secret Life of Pets*.

When the Academy Award nominations for 2019 were announced, the producers of *Spider-Man: Into the Spider-Verse* found themselves facing fierce competition. Two Disney animated films, *Incredibles 2* and *Ralph Breaks the Internet*, had garnered huge audiences—*Incredibles 2* eventually earned more than $1.2 billion, and *Ralph Breaks the Internet* earned more than $500 million in worldwide ticket sales. But many critics predicted *Spider-Man: Into the Spider-Verse* would ultimately claim the Academy Award. CNN entertainment writer Brian Lowry asserted that "Disney actually released a pair of excellent [films] in *Incredibles 2* and *Ralph Breaks the Internet*, but the dazzling animation of this . . . feature possessed a freshness that they inevitably lacked, and should complete its triumphant swing through awards season."[16]

As Lowry and other critics predicted, when the votes were counted the Academy Award went to *Spider-Man: Into the Spider-*

Miguel Jiron, one the chief animators on Spider-Man: Into the Spider-Verse, *is considered a rising star in animation. The film merged traditional hand-drawn animation techniques with digital technology, an effect that won over audiences and earned the film an Academy Award.*

Verse. Although many factors contributed to the success of the film—among them the riveting story and voice-over work by the actors—critics cited the animators for their achievements as well. According to *New York Times* critic A.O. Scott,

> The characters feel liberated by the animation, and the audience will, too. Old-style graphic techniques commingle with digital wizardry. Wiggly lines indicate the tingling of spider senses, while electronic bursts signal the presence of interdimensional static. The rules of visual coherence are tested and ultimately upheld, while the laws of physics are flouted with sublime bravado.[17]

Thanks to his work on *Spider-Man: Into the Spider-Verse*, Jiron is recognized as one of the industry's rising stars. He urges young animators to create their own unique styles. He says, "I've found that having a unique point of view and personal sensibility that rings loud and clear in your work is even more important than your portfolio. Not only will your personal work reflect you and your voice, it's also the fastest way of learning skill and craft."[18]

Niki Lindroth von Bahr and the Art of Stop-Motion

Stop-motion animation dates back to the late 1800s, when filmmakers discovered they could make characters come alive on film by building miniature models of the characters, then photographing them one frame at a time. After the movie camera shoots a single frame of film, crew members step into the scene and move each model's arms, legs, and other parts of their bodies ever so slightly. Then the photographer shoots another frame—and on and on until the film is finished. It is a slow, tedious process, but the technique was used to make a giant ape come to life in the 1933 film *King Kong*; a sea monster terrorize New York City in the 1953 film *The Beast from 20,000 Fathoms*; and skeletons battle Greek heroes in a sword fight in the 1963 film *Jason and the Argonauts*.

Production of stop-motion films has continued into the twenty-first century; however, with the domination of CGI, fewer animators are turning to the technique. Swedish animator Niki Lindroth von Bahr hopes to reverse the trend. Working with puppets as the stars of her films, Lindroth von Bahr has produced numerous highly acclaimed stop-motion films. Among her achievements is *The Burden*, a fourteen-minute animated film that features singing and dancing animals—although the film is hardly lighthearted fare. Indeed, the troubled characters tell dark stories through their songs, much of which have to do with the anxiety they face in their low-paying, dead-end jobs. Lindroth von Bahr says many audience members can certainly identify with the characters. "I've also worked a lot [of] really, really depressing and pointless jobs to make money, because most of us need to from time to time,"[19] she says. *The Burden* won first place in the 2017 International Animation Film Festival in Annecy, France.

As an art and theater student during the first decade of the twenty-first century, Lindroth von Bahr originally intended to work in live theater and film, studying set and prop design at the Scandinavian School for Stage Designers in Skelleftea, Sweden. But she eventually found herself drawn to animation. She says, "I actually started out by studying prop making for film and theatre. I've always been very interested in materials and wanted to build the sets and puppets for my own films. That, combined with my love for narrative and telling a good story, got me into the stop-motion animation business."[20]

"I've always been very interested in materials and wanted to build the sets and puppets for my own films."[20]

—Animator Niki Lindroth von Bahr

Lasseter, Twomey, Jiron, and Lindroth von Bahr have worked in diverse areas of animation—from CGI to cel animation to stop-motion filmmaking. Nevertheless, their work all qualifies as animation, illustrating how different styles of the art continue to find legions of dedicated fans throughout the world.

CHAPTER THREE

New Outlets for Animation

Artists have had limited options for reaching their audiences and showcasing their talents during much of animation's history. Movie studios and theaters tightly controlled the animator's art during the industry's golden age. By the 1950s, television had added a new audience, but the studios and television networks still exerted control over the work of the artists. During the early twenty-first century, the market for animation has grown, with a myriad of opportunities for artists to showcase their work. Not only has the number of animation outlets increased, but the artists have pushed the edge of experimental animation to new levels as well.

One familiar showcase for experimental animation is the Internet, where the animation known as the GIF appeared early on and has continued to be a presence. Indeed, everyone who has ever surfed the Internet has seen them, and even though they are short and often annoying, they are ubiquitous on the web. The GIF—the acronym stands for "Graphics Interchange Format"—was the first form of animation to appear on the Internet. An animated GIF is basically a series of still pictures that are displayed, in color and without sound, sequentially on a user's Internet browser. Most GIFs are looped, so that they play over and over, with no way for the user to stop them. Animated GIFs range from tiny moving graphic images to short videos that display any subject imaginable.

The GIF is but one format available to today's animators. Thanks to the Internet, other formats—and various avenues for

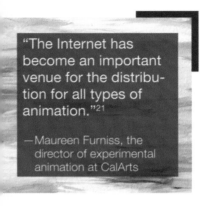

reaching audiences—have opened to artists. According to Maureen Furniss, an author and director of experimental animation at CalArts, "The Internet has become an important venue for the distribution for all types of animation, including short animated works. Because of it, every animation creator can exhibit his or her films to a potential audience, and can find others who share common interests."[21]

Large studios such as Disney and DreamWorks Animation still dominate theatrically released animated films. But independent animators can take advantage of websites such as YouTube and Vimeo, which give them the space they need to display their creativity.

YouTube and Vimeo

YouTube was founded in 2005 as a video-hosting service by three former employees of PayPal, the website that enables users to pay for goods and services through an online process. Beginning with the first video upload (a short clip of one of the founders visiting a zoo), YouTube has grown into a global Internet phenomenon. By 2018, it had 1.9 billion monthly users. Every day some 5 billion videos are watched by viewers around the world. Among those videos is content of every conceivable nature, from documentary films and instructional videos to music videos and clips from TV shows. YouTube is also the largest outlet for animation on the Internet, with hundreds if not thousands of channels devoted specifically to animation.

Although the largest of the online video sites, YouTube was not the first video-hosting site. Vimeo was founded in November 2004, just a few months before YouTube went online. The site was started by two filmmakers looking for a way to present their films to an audience. Today Vimeo has some 170 million viewers each month who watch more than 700 million videos.

An artist in China works on an animated program that will debut on YouTube. YouTube has become the largest outlet for animation on the Internet.

Animators can earn money on these sites on the basis of the total number of views and number of subscribers to their channels. These video-hosting services allow animators great flexibility in their productions, not only in content but also in running time. A two-minute animation that would never be acceptable for traditional television broadcast can find a welcome home on the Internet.

Internet Animation Artists

Alex Clark is among the animation artists who have found a home on YouTube. Clark has traveled the world as a comedian, juggler, and street performer. He grew up fascinated with the animated Disney movie *Aladdin*, which would ultimately change his life. "I've been lucky to perform in seven-plus countries, but was always bummed that as soon as the show was over, the audience was gone," he says. "That's when I found YouTube and

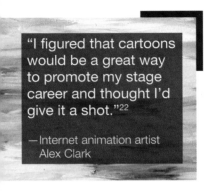

remembered how much I loved animation as a kid. I figured that cartoons would be a great way to promote my stage career and thought I'd give it a shot."[22]

That shot resulted in his animated series *It's Alex Clark*, which appears on Clark's YouTube channel. The series has more than 3 million subscribers who follow the humorous animated videos that portray episodes from Clark's life. For Clark, having YouTube as a creative outlet is a boon for the animation community. "I love seeing how diverse the YouTube community is," he says. "Some people run their channel as a one-man shop, and others turn it into a respected multi-million dollar company. So my favorite part is that there are no barriers to entry except for yourself."[23]

Tom Ridgewell, known on YouTube as TomSka, is a British filmmaker, writer, and the creator of short animated sketches that draw millions of viewers to his YouTube channel. Ridgewell chose to put his animations on YouTube rather than find a broadcast television outlet for his work. "For me," he says, "TV doesn't offer enough. Not enough freedom. . . . It's more fun here. If I mess up in my house I won't get fired, I can take risks." His comedy series, *Crash Zoom*, features the misadventures of three animated characters, Ben, Lucy, and Kate. Ridgewell acknowledges that competition is fierce on YouTube. "Everyone is on YouTube now," he says. "You've got to really work to keep up your game."[24]

Streaming Animation on Netflix

While animation has flourished on services such as Vimeo and YouTube, mainstream Internet-based streaming services have also become a popular outlet for twenty-first-century animation. These services, which include Netflix, Hulu, Amazon Prime, and Apple TV+, are worldwide platforms that offer animated films and series from a variety of sources, both domestic and international.

Streaming animation can be watched anytime and anywhere on numerous devices, from TVs and tablets to laptops and smartphones. Users are required to pay monthly fees to access the streaming services.

Netflix, the oldest of the streaming services, was established in 1997. Today it has nearly 150 million users in some 190 countries around the world. It has become so popular that many TV remote controls feature a Netflix button for easy access to the service. In partnership with such major studios as DreamWorks Animation and Hasbro, Netflix is a major outlet for feature-length films and series aimed at young people.

Animating for Virtual Reality

The immersive world of virtual reality (VR) has created a new outlet for animation. By donning a VR headset, a viewer enters an artificial world and can move about and interact with that world. Video games, music concerts, and films—both live action and animated—are well suited to the unique environment produced by VR. Among the popular animated shows produced for VR viewing is a series titled *Alex's Sci-Fi World*, created by animator Matt Schaefer. This futuristic world features street scenes filled with aliens, monsters, robots, space vehicles, and graffiti-covered buildings.

Creating images for VR requires animators to employ skills they would not use in TV or movie animation. Animation on a TV or movie screen is known as linear animation, meaning the images move directly in front of the audience in a linear path. In VR, though, the images may come at the viewer from any angle. Therefore, the animator must compose the art so that it changes in size, shape, and perspective as the image moves, for example, from a far corner of the viewer's eyesight to a linear position directly in front of the viewer. "The biggest difference between VR and linear projects is that you are putting yourself inside the experience and looking at the animation with this new perspective," says Jake Rowell, the creative director for Wevr, a studio that produces animated shows for the VR market. "This participation gives you a lot to think about and react to with regards to scale and speed of movement."

Quoted in Ian Failes, "Animation in a VR World: How Is It Different and How Is It the Same?," CartoonBrew, April 12, 2017. www.cartoonbrew.com.

In 2018 Netflix launched a new animation division to produce original animated content aimed at family audiences. The number and variety of projects slated for production provide work for some of the most talented and high-profile animators. "We're trying to take the Netflix philosophy of empowering creators and bring that into the animation space," says Melissa Cobb, the head of family animation projects for Netflix. "We're not focused on creating a singular brand identity. We want to produce a broad range of content that appeals to kids and families all over the world. . . . We're just at the very beginning of that process, but I'm sure we will continue to find new ways for kids to interact with the characters they love from Netflix shows."[25] The animated films and series will employ a wide range of animation methods, including CGI and stop-motion.

"We're trying to take the Netflix philosophy of empowering creators and bring that into the animation space."[25]

—Melissa Cobb, the head of family animation projects for Netflix

Among the projects under development for Netflix is a new version of the Pinocchio story involving a puppet that comes to life. This time, the story will be set against the backdrop of Fascist Italy during the years leading up to World War II. Also under development is *Over the Moon*, a fantasy about a girl who boards a rocket ship to find a lunar goddess; *Kid Cosmic*, a series about a nine-year-old boy with superpowers; and *My Father's Dragon*, an animated feature produced by Nora Twomey that focuses on a young boy's quest to find a fire-breathing dragon. Meanwhile, animator Jorge R. Gutiérrez (known for his work on several acclaimed animated TV series) is producing a nine-episode limited series titled *Maya and the Three* that tells the story of a warrior princess. It is expected to debut in 2021. "I've worked in a lot of places," says Gutiérrez. "Every time I went to a studio they'd talk about the legacy they'd established during a golden era some 30 or 50 years ago. The appeal of Netflix is there is no legacy. This is the golden era, and I get to be a part of building this foundation."[26]

Alternative Settings for Animation

Work by contemporary animators like Gutiérrez can be found in movie theaters or on television or computer screens, but the art of animation has broken free of the typical venues, leading to new ways to experience animation. Seeing a movie in a theater requires viewers to sit in a seat facing a screen on which the film is projected. While usually enjoyable, it is a passive experience. New and cutting-edge animation installations take the film out of the theater and into the world at large, creating a new dynamic between the viewer and the work being viewed. These site-specific films are not traditional animations like cartoons but are instead visual experiences brought into the real world. They may be projected, for example, on buildings or other large structures, and they may have a particular relevance to the location being used. For example, the German design collective Urbanscreen has projected animations on such diverse locations as the roof of the Sydney Opera House in Australia and a 400-foot-tall (122 m) gas tank in Germany.

In Brazil, filmmaker and animation artist Fernando Salis used site-specific animation on one of Rio de Janeiro's most famous landmarks: the Christ the Redeemer statue that stands 98 feet (30 m) tall on a Brazilian mountaintop. Using projected animation and other images, Salis seemingly made the statue come to life, its outstretched arms appearing to fold inward in an all-encompassing hug. The program, which ran for two nights, was part of a Brazilian campaign aimed at raising awareness of abuse of children and teenagers.

Site-specific installations are not limited to exterior use; many theatrical plays have used animation as a part of their scenic design. In 2019, a stage production of the 1997 animated film *Anastasia* toured the country. The story recounts the adventures of a young princess who escapes the 1917 revolution in Russia. The stage version featured live singers and dancers, of course, but also a generous amount of CGI projected onto the background of the scenes. Jim Rutter, the theater critic for the *Philadelphia Inquirer*, wrote, "What a backdrop this production brought on tour. [Set designer] Alexander Dodge fills the huge panels of his scenic

A projected animation created by the Urbanscreen design collective illuminates a wall of the European Central Bank in Frankfurt, Germany. Buildings and other structures provide alternative settings for cutting-edge animation installations.

Streaming the *Peanuts* Gang

Technology giant Apple announced in 2019 its launch of Apple TV+, a new Internet-based entertainment streaming service. And, very quickly, executives at Apple said they would join their competitors—Hulu, Netflix, and Amazon Prime—in programming animated shows. In fact, soon after announcing the launch of the streaming service, Apple disclosed plans to stream an animated series featuring the characters from the *Peanuts* comic strip: Charlie Brown, Linus, Lucy, Snoopy, Woodstock, and others.

Peanuts was created by cartoonist Charles M. Schulz in 1950 and was published for decades in daily newspapers, many of which continue to publish his original comic strips long after his death in 2000. In 1965 the characters came to life in an animated special, *A Charlie Brown Christmas*, which produced rave reviews among TV critics. According to TV critic Simon Abrams, "[Charlie Brown's] struggle to find meaning during the holiday season is very relatable, and probably one of the most moving programs that mainstream television has produced." Since then, some forty TV specials featuring the *Peanuts* characters have aired on broadcast TV. The decision by Apple to stream the *Peanuts* series illustrates how streaming services have established themselves as a new home for animated entertainment.

Simon Abrams, "All 45 Peanuts Specials, Ranked," Vulture, November 22, 2018. www.vulture.com.

design with as much computer-generated imagery as a Pixar film. Snow falls lightly on a czarist palace, a harsh sun beats down on the columns of the Nevsky Prospect, wind ruffles the clouds above the Seine in Paris."[27]

On the Festival Circuit

Audiences searching for unusual and unique animation experiences not ordinarily found on television or in movie theaters can often find them at film festivals. Such festivals are common and are often staged in major cities, although small towns feature them as well. There are thousands of film festivals around the world, including many that serve as qualifying venues for the Academy

Awards. And many film festivals are devoted entirely to screening new animated features.

The world's largest animation festival is the Annecy International Animation Film Festival in Annecy, France. Established in 1960, it was the first film festival strictly devoted to animation. During the annual festival, animators compete in various categories, including feature films, short films, films for television and advertising, Internet films, and student films. By entering the festival, animators have the opportunity to present their work not only to audiences but also to film industry executives who can arrange to finance, promote, and distribute the work.

In 2018 animator Denis Do's film *Funan* won the festival's top prize for an animated feature, the Cristal. The film, set in war-torn Cambodia in 1975, tells the story of a mother who is separated from her son by the oppressive, brutal regime known as the Khmer Rouge and how she gains the courage to find him. The woman in Do's film is based on his own mother. Peter Debruge, the film critic for *Variety* magazine, writes,

> How does one depict a genocide such as that inflicted by the Khmer Rouge on the Cambodian people? . . . By embracing hand-drawn animation as a tool for tactful re-creation, *Funan* director Denis Do provides audiences a unique window into this relatively under-represented 20th-century horror, one that serves as an act of witnessing even as it avoids directly showing the violence on-screen.[28]

There are more than fifty animation festivals in America, including the Los Angeles International Film Festival; the Florida Animation Festival in Tallahassee; the Khem Animation Film Festival in Woodbridge, New Jersey; and the Eyeworks Festival of Experimental Animation, which is held over the course of three weekends in Los Angeles, Chicago, and New York City. In addition, the Walt Disney Family Museum Teen Animation Festival

Animators connect with others in the industry at the Annecy International Animation Film Festival in France—the largest such festival in the world. Winning a competition at festivals like this one can launch an animator's career.

International in San Francisco gives teen animators from around the world a chance to screen their animated films.

Aside from animators being able to showcase their films, they find the festivals are important places to network and learn from their peers. Animators can be a reclusive bunch, staring at computer screens or drawing boards for hours on end. But even the shyest animators can connect with others at a festival, and perhaps even meet one of the stars of the animation world.

It is likely that many of these young animators have been posting their work on their own YouTube and Vimeo channels. But if their work is good enough to be accepted for a major animation festival, the experience can lead to mass-market platforms for their work. This could include big animation studios such as Hasbro, Disney, and DreamWorks Animation—all of which still have influence in the animation world.

CHAPTER FOUR

The Changing Roles of Women in Animation

Lisa Hanawalt started drawing pictures of birds in high school. Mostly, she enjoyed drawing comical sketches of toucans—long-beaked birds found in the tropical rain forests of South America. Eventually, Hanawalt created a character she called Tuca. "I created her after watching a nature documentary about toucans where they were, like, poking their beaks into other birds' nests to steal the eggs and gobble them," says Hanawalt. "So the birds were creating these nests that were longer and longer, in order to avoid the toucans stealing their young, basically. And I thought that was so funny. Like, toucans are so selfish and greedy, I really related to it. They're so naughty. It's so funny to me."[29]

The cel-animated series *Tuca & Bertie* debuted on Netflix in 2019. The show, which was created by Hanawalt, features two birds as the main characters: Tuca, the cocky, carefree toucan Hanawalt first envisioned in high school, and Bertie, a shy, reserved songbird. "I put my worst behavior traits into this fictional bird character called Tuca," says Hanawalt. "Bertie is a nice counterpoint to her."[30]

After tuning in, viewers of *Tuca & Bertie* will immediately realize the show is not centered in a tropical rain forest but rather in a big city. The show explores the lives of the two young birds (who, in another reality, could easily be two young women) sharing

> "I put my worst behavior traits into this fictional bird character called Tuca. Bertie is a nice counterpoint to her."[30]
>
> —Animator Lisa Hanawalt

an apartment. They endure life together, along with its squabbles, challenges, and triumphs. "It's sort of a soothing show to watch," says Hanawalt. "Very relaxing and sweet and funny and feels friendly, like these are your buddies, but also . . . there are some darker themes that are touched on in the show. I want it grounded in things that I worry about from day to day."[31]

Hanawalt's success in bringing *Tuca & Bertie* to Netflix illustrates how women are finding successful careers in animation. Yet it has not always been that way. For decades, many women found it difficult to establish careers as professional animators. In

Lisa Hanawalt (center) created the new Netflix cel-animated series Tuca & Bertie. *Her characters, two bird women in their thirties who live in the same building and share their lives, are voiced by Tiffany Haddish (left) and Ali Wong (right).*

fact, the advocacy group Women in Animation (WIA) reports that women hold just 20 percent of the jobs in the American animation industry. Many women who work in animation say the industry is similar to other creative professions in that it has long been dominated by men. Female animators have encountered the glass ceiling found in other industries. Animator Nina Gantz says, "I found it intimidating at the beginning."[32]

Gantz was able to overcome the intimidation she encountered when she first entered the animation profession. A native of

Romeo and Juliet in Stop-Motion Animation

Romeo and Juliet is one of William Shakespeare's best-known plays. First performed on stage in 1597, it is a tragedy that tells of the ill-fated love between teens Romeo and Juliet amid the conflicts caused by their warring families, the Montagues and the Capulets. Over the centuries *Romeo and Juliet* has remained a staple of live theater. It has also been filmed numerous times as a live-action movie, the most recent version of which was released in 2013.

A 1913 version of Shakespeare's tragedy marked a milestone in animation. It was produced that year by animator Helena Smith Dayton, who filmed clay puppets in her stop-motion version of the play.

Sadly, copies of Dayton's stop-motion movie of *Romeo and Juliet* have all been lost. Other stop-motion productions by Dayton have been lost as well. But film historian Jason Cody Douglass was able to unearth news accounts written about her work. Douglass has found that the film critics of a century ago generally raved about the quality of Dayton's work. He says,

> As a trained dancer and financially successful sculptor of human models, Dayton likely depended upon her eye for form and flow to develop an aesthetic [for] fluid movement. And the fruits of her labor were not overlooked. As early as March 25, 1917, just after a screening of Dayton's "animated sculpture films" at New York's Strand Theater, reviewers began to make note of Dayton's characters "jumping about as if they were real."

Jason Cody Douglass, "Helena Smith Dayton: An Early Animation Pioneer Whose Films You Have Never Seen," *Animation Studies 2.0* (blog), September 24, 2018. https://blog.animationstudies.org.

Rotterdam in the Netherlands, Gantz produced the stop-motion animated film *Edmond*, which has been awarded prizes by the Sundance Film Festival as well as the British Academy of Film and Television Arts.

Disney Once Barred Women

Still, as Gantz and other female animators suggest, for many years the doors of the animation studios remained closed to women. In fact, in the earliest days of the Disney studio, the studio bosses prohibited women from holding creative jobs. "Women do not do any of the creative work in connection with preparing the cartoons for the screen, as that work is performed entirely by young men," a Disney employment brochure explained to prospective employees. "The only work open to women consists of tracing the characters on clear celluloid sheets with India ink and filling in the tracings on the reverse side with paint according to directions."[33]

> "The only work open to women consists of tracing the characters on clear celluloid sheets with India ink and filling in the tracings on the reverse side with paint according to directions."[33]
>
> —An early Disney studio employment brochure

As that brochure states, women were allowed to hold positions in the Ink and Paint Department, where—years before computers took over the job—they were assigned the tedious task of hand coloring the thousands of animation cels needed for each film. Even though women who worked in the Ink and Paint Department were barred from working in the studio's creative positions, some women did stand out in the department. During the 1930s, for example, Mary Weiser found a job in the Ink and Paint Department. In her spare time, she studied chemistry and developed the first paints and inks specifically formulated to provide color to animation cels. In 1932, before Weiser's pioneering work in chemistry, animators were limited to just some eighty shades of the three primary colors: red, yellow, and blue. Five years later, thanks to Weiser's research, animators could draw from a palette of some fifteen hundred colors. In fact, many of the colors developed by Weiser first showed up on the screen in Disney's 1937 production of *Snow White and the Seven Dwarfs*.

Although women were barred from creative jobs at Disney, other studios were willing to give women the opportunities to show their creative talents. During the late 1920s and early 1930s, Lillian Friedman worked for the Max Fleischer Studio, where she animated cartoons featuring the characters Popeye and Betty Boop. In 1933 she was promoted to head animator at the studio. Eunice Macaulay's career in animation started during the 1940s, working in the Ink and Paint Department at the Gaumont British Animation studio. She was eventually promoted into creative positions and worked on more than twenty-five animated features into the 1980s. Her 1978 animated short, *Special Delivery*, won the Academy Award for Best Animated Short Film. Another Academy Award winner was Faith Hubley, who, along with her husband, John Hubley, established the independent animation company Storybook Studios. Faith Hubley went on to win two Academy Awards: the 1962 prize for the cartoon *A Herb Alpert & the Tijuana Brass Double Feature* and the 1966 trophy for the cartoon *The Hole*.

Meanwhile, by the 1950s, the studio bosses at Disney had finally dropped the rule against hiring women for creative positions in the animation department. One of the first women to find a successful career as an animator at Disney was Elizabeth Case Zwicker, who served as one of the chief animators on the 1959 film *Sleeping Beauty*. She later recalled, "I did birds in *Sleeping Beauty*. I studied how birds fly in the research library. I developed a bird consciousness. Then I did the jester with striped sleeves, the stripes are very difficult."[34]

Once the film was finished, Disney laid off the animators—a common practice in the industry years ago. (Typically, anima-

> "I did birds in *Sleeping Beauty*. I studied how birds fly in the research library. I developed a bird consciousness."[34]
>
> —Disney animator Elizabeth Case Zwicker

tors would find themselves out of work between projects.) As for Zwicker, even though she worked on one of Disney's most successful and highly praised animated features, she was never able to find another job in the animation industry. Afterward, she earned her living as a commercial illustrator.

Helping Women Overcome Bias

Under the Civil Rights Act of 1964, US employers are barred from exercising gender discrimination in the workplace. This means that if a studio issued an employment brochure announcing that it would not hire women for creative roles in its animation department—as Disney did during the 1930s—the studio would be in violation of federal law. Moreover, California's Fair Employment and Housing Act—adopted in 1959—also bars gender discrimination in the workplace. And since many animation studios are located in California, such discrimination would also violate state law.

Still, as the statistics compiled by WIA illustrate, although discrimination on the basis of gender is illegal, progress has been slow in convincing studio bosses to hire and promote women. According to WIA, just 10 percent of the jobs of animation producers and directors are held by women. It means professionals like Hanawalt—a woman who has created and oversees the production of an animated series or feature film—are rare. In addition, according to WIA statistics, only 17 percent of the writers working in animation are women, and only 23 percent of the actual animators—the professionals who produce the cels, stop-motion effects, or the CGI images—are women. Marge Dean, the copresident of WIA, says, "The first thing we're asked when we share these startling statistics is 'How does this happen? Why does this happen?' And the next question is 'How do we change it?'"[35]

Attracting Big Audiences

Despite their uphill climb into the creative roles at animation studios, many women have achieved success in animation, particularly in the animated series and features that have attracted big audiences. For example, Nora Smith has worked as a producer, writer, and animator for the Fox network's weekly animated series *Bob's Burgers*, a comedy centered at the Belcher family's seaside hamburger restaurant. During her tenure at *Bob's Burgers*, Smith has been nominated four times for an Emmy Award—the TV industry's highest honor. In 2017 she won the Outstanding Animated Program Emmy as the show's executive producer. Moreover, in 2018, Apple TV+ streaming service announced its hiring of Smith to serve as an animation consultant for the series *Central Park*, a musical comedy that tells how a family of caretakers in New York's sprawling public park becomes involved in an adventure to save the planet from destruction.

Meanwhile, the Amazon Prime streaming service announced in 2018 its choice of producer Kate Purdy to helm its new animated series *Undone*, a drama that tells the story of a young woman named Alma who escapes from a near-fatal automobile accident. After emerging from the accident, Alma discovers she has the ability to travel through time—a power she uses to understand the uncomfortable truths she discovers about herself, her friends, and family members.

Nora Smith has worked as a producer, writer, and animator for Fox Network's animated series Bob's Burgers. *Her work on the show, which revolves around a family-run seaside hamburger restaurant (pictured), has earned industry acclaim.*

Women in Animation's 50/50 by 2025 Initiative

The advocacy group Women in Animation (WIA) has undertaken the 50/50 by 2025 initiative—a project to ensure that by the year 2025, women will hold 50 percent of the jobs in the American animation industry. To achieve the goal of equality in the animation industry, the organization lobbies studio bosses on behalf of female animators, hoping to help unlock doors for them. Moreover, WIA holds workshops for female animators, helping them recognize bias and formulate strategies to convince studio bosses that they are capable of holding important jobs in the industry. WIA has also established a mentorship program, pairing successful female animators with young women seeking to gain a foothold in the profession. And WIA sponsors a scholarship program for female students aspiring to careers in animation.

Producer Rosa Tran, who was nominated for an Academy Award for her work on the 2015 stop-motion animated film *Anomalisa*, comments, "My advice to a young woman getting into animation today is to believe in yourself. . . . Don't wait for anybody to hand you anything. Don't be afraid to toot your own horn and say 'I'm interested in doing this,' or 'I'd like to be a part of that project with you. I'm capable and I have these skills. . . . I can do anything.'"

Quoted in Terry Flores, "Women in Animation Leads Push to Get More Females into the Toon Business," *Variety*, February 4, 2016. https://variety.com.

Another animator who has found wide success is Rebecca Sugar, the creator of the cel-animated science fiction series *Steven Universe*, which has been featured on Cartoon Network since 2013. She also worked as a storyboard artist for the cel-animated series *Adventure Time*, which tells the story of a young boy with magical powers that aired from 2010 to 2013 on the Cartoon Network. As a storyboard artist, Sugar was responsible for sketching each scene of the story by following the script, which the animators used as a guide to create the cels filmed for the production. Sugar also worked as a storyboard artist for the 2012 stop-motion film comedy *Hotel Transylvania*.

Noelle Stevenson is the producer of the Netflix animated series *She-Ra and the Princesses of Power*—a reboot of the 1980s-era series about a mythical princess with superhuman strength and speed. While still attending the Maryland Institute College of Art—where she graduated with a degree in illustration

Noelle Stevenson is the producer of the Netflix series She-Ra and the Princesses of Power. *She says the series is one of the few animated action shows that features women in lead roles.*

in 2013—Stevenson found success as an artist. As a student she created an online graphic novel, *Nimona*, which is a science fiction tale about the young, do-gooding assistant to an evil mad scientist. Warner Bros. plans to release an animated version of Stevenson's web-based comic in 2020.

Meanwhile, though, Stevenson has brought the cel-animated *She-Ra* back to life. "I've always been hungry for fantasy and sci-fi that heavily featured women," says Stevenson. "*She-Ra* was ahead of its time in that sense, and we still don't see action-adventure with female leads nearly as much as I would like these days. That's starting to change, which is very exciting. It's the perfect moment for *She-Ra* to return."[36]

A New Godzilla

Joining animators such as Smith, Purdy, Sugar, and Stevenson as important figures in the animation industry is Alexandra Bernier, who directed the CGI effects for a new film featuring Godzilla. When the producers of a sequel to the 1954 film *Godzilla* decided to create a new saga surrounding the huge, scary sea monster, they opted to go full bore into CGI rather than follow the original and employ an actor to stomp through a miniaturized version of Tokyo wearing a lizard suit. The 2019 version, *Godzilla: King of the Monsters*, reportedly cost $200 million to produce. Overseeing the animation for this colossal Hollywood undertaking was veteran CGI visual effects director Bernier, whose other Hollywood credits include supervisory CGI work on such films as *Shazam!*, *The Predator*, *The Greatest Showman*, *Jumanji: Welcome to the Jungle*, *Justice League*, *Wonder Woman*, *Pirates of the Caribbean: Dead Men Tell No Tales*, and *X-Men: Apocalypse*.

In the more than sixty years since the actor wearing the lizard costume traipsed through downtown Tokyo in the original *Godzilla*, there have been some thirty sequels featuring the sea monster produced by movie studios in the United States and Japan. Over the years, these sequels have employed the ever-changing techniques of animation, including productions that featured stop-motion, cel animation, and CGI. Critics who got an early look at the 2019 version raved about the quality of the CGI produced under Bernier's direction. Critic Adam Holmes wrote on the website CinemaBlend,

> Godzilla's been keeping a low profile in the MonsterVerse since 2014, but . . . he's jumping back into action for *Godzilla: King of the Monsters*. This time around, the giant reptile is colliding with [monsters] Rodan, Mothra and, arguably the most dangerous of them all, the three-headed King Ghidorah. That last monster is described as Godzilla's "ultimate nemesis," meaning he needs to be especially terrifying, and thankfully, the latest picture of Ghidorah in *King of the Monsters* gives off just that kind of vibe.
>
> King Ghidorah first appeared in 1964's *Ghidorah, the Three-Headed Monster* and has been a regular player in Japan's monster movie scene, but *Godzilla: King of the Monsters* marks his first appearance in American cinema. Thanks to the wonders of CGI . . . Ghidorah is the most fearsome he's ever looked. Granted, you don't want to be near any of these monsters, but Ghidorah is definitely one of the ones that means to threaten humanity.[37]

The work of animators such as Alexandra Bernier, Kate Purdy, Nora Smith, Rebecca Sugar, Nina Gantz, and Lisa Hanawalt are being noticed by critics as well as audiences, who enjoy their work immensely. These women and others are carving out important careers for themselves in the art of animation, showing they have the talent and creativity to produce cutting-edge entertainment.

CHAPTER FIVE

The Future of Animation

In 1994 the Disney studio released the animated film *The Lion King* to theaters. The film tells the story of a lion cub named Simba who overcomes the evil intentions of the villainous lion Scar to eventually rule over the animal kingdom in Africa. The film became one of Disney's most successful animated features, earning more than $900 million in worldwide ticket sales. Moreover, several of the film's songs, written by pop music superstar Elton John, went on to be hits. The film won two Academy Awards as well as the Golden Globe Award for Best Motion Picture—Musical or Comedy. And, in 1997, an extravagant musical play based on the animated film opened on Broadway in New York City.

The Lion King was produced through cel animation. In fact, the filmmakers commenced work on the project in 1991 when the director, Roger Allers, traveled to East Africa with a team of animators and artists. The purpose of the trip was to get a first-hand look at the environment they planned to reproduce on animation cels. "What a day, when our guide brought us to the top of a bluff, and it was as if you could see forever," recalls production designer Chris Sanders. "The air was clear and you looked out across valleys and mountains and canyons. It was all dappled with sunlight and shadow and you could take in so much at once that we could see five separate thunderstorms moving through the landscape at one time."[38]

The animators spent the next three years reproducing those colorful images, which were rendered on animation cells both by

The original version of Disney's The Lion King *(pictured) featured traditional cel animation. The new animated film, produced through CGI, features remarkably lifelike animals.*

hand and computer through the CAPS procedure. Critics found many reasons to praise the film, but the animators were often singled out for their achievements. *New York Times* film critic Janet Maslin wrote, "Together with a vibrant palette and grandly scenic African landscapes, these elements give the best of *The Lion King* a bright, energetic appeal."[39]

A new version of *The Lion King* was released by Disney in 2019. Unlike the original cel-animated version, the 2019 version was produced through CGI. Animation experts were stunned by advance scenes of the new version: although no live actors or, certainly, animals were filmed to produce the new version, the characters appear to be lifelike in every sense—from the twitching whiskers of the newborn Simba to Scar's angry scowls. After viewing the advance scenes, entertainment journalist Josh Weiss wrote, "Even with such a limited amount of footage, it's not hard to see that this is going to be one gorgeous piece of filmmaking. . . . [Director Jon] Favreau is bringing the African Savannah to vivid life in a way that [cel] animation never could."[40]

The Realm of Photorealism

By employing the computer to create the artwork, the filmmakers seek to take animation into the realm of photorealism. Photorealism strives to create animated images that appear so lifelike that audiences would see no difference between live characters filmed with a conventional camera and animated characters created by a computer. According to technology writer Nicolae Sfetcu,

> Eventually, the goal is to create software where the animator can generate a movie sequence showing a photorealistic human character, undergoing physically-plausible motion, together with clothes, photorealistic hair, a complicated natural background, and possibly interacting with other simulated human characters. This should be done in a way that the viewer is no longer able to tell if a particular movie sequence is computer-generated, or created using real actors in front of movie cameras.[41]

Although films like the 2019 version of *The Lion King* try to set new standards for using CGI to create a photorealistic effect, many prior films have employed these techniques. Many of these have mixed CGI images with live actors. For example, in 2001 the first film in the widely popular *The Fast and the Furious* series debuted. The series includes plenty of cops, crooks, and car chases. By 2019, the eight films in the series had reaped more than $1.5 billion at the box office. Three more films in the series are planned through 2021.

During the production of the seventh film in the series, *Furious 7*, one of movie's stars, actor Paul Walker, died in a car accident (unrelated to the filming). To complete the 2015 movie, the filmmakers hired Walker's brothers Caleb and Cody as body doubles, meaning they took their brother's place in several of the movie's scenes. Audiences could not tell the difference, though, because the filmmakers employed CGI to digitally alter the appearances of the two brothers, essentially changing the faces of Caleb and Cody so it appeared as though Walker was featured in the scenes.

Although the filmmakers successfully fooled audiences into believing Walker was featured in the entire movie, critics wondered whether it was the right path to take. They suggested it may not be socially acceptable to create animated images of an actor who is no longer alive. Entertainment journalist Meghan Chou writes, "Some people congratulated [the animators] for preserving Walker's legacy, while others felt queasy watching this digital rendering of the actor."[42] Chou points out that other producers soon followed this technique. For example, the 2016 *Star Wars* sequel *Rogue One* included scenes featuring actor Peter Cushing, who appeared as the villain Grand Moff Tarkin in the original 1977 *Star Wars* film. But by the time the 2016 sequel was released, Cushing had already been dead for twenty-two years.

For the sequel, the producers enlisted actor Guy Henry to walk through the role of Grand Moff Tarkin. Henry even spoke the scripted dialogue. But then the animators took over, using CGI to digitally alter Henry's face with animated images of Cushing. John Knoll, the visual effects supervisor for *Rogue One*, defended the filmmakers' decision to resurrect a deceased actor using CGI. "We weren't doing anything that I think Peter Cushing would've objected to," he said. "I think this work was done with

Animation Through Motion Capture

One way in which filmmakers merge animated characters into live-action films is through the process known as motion capture, in which an actor plays a scene wearing a special suit that records digital signals on film. The signals may be conveyed through lights embedded in the suit or even through white dots painted on the garment. After the scene is filmed, an animated character created on a computer can be laid atop the image of the actor in the motion-capture suit. In the final version, the live actor is replaced by the animated character—who follows all the physical motions expressed by the actor during the original filming. Thus, the motions of the actor are captured by the computer.

Motion capture was used to produce the three films in the *Ted* series, which tells the story of a toy teddy bear who comes to life and provides a wisecracking, pot-smoking companion to his boyhood owner (who has grown into adulthood). The main character, Ted, is portrayed by actor and director Seth MacFarlane. To portray the character of Ted, MacFarlane wore a motion-capture suit in his scenes with live actors. McFarlane says, "Everything had to be treated exactly as it would be treated for a live actor, and it really makes a huge difference; it really brings Ted into that world. You don't feel like he's the one element that was inserted after the fact; it feels like he was there from the very beginning."

Quoted in Matt Barone, "Interview: Seth MacFarlane Talks *Ted*, Realistic CGI Movie Characters, and Keeping *Family Guy* Relevant," *Complex*, June 5, 2012. www.complex.com.

a great deal of affection and care. We know that Peter Cushing was very proud of his involvement in *Star Wars* and had said as much, and that he regretted that he never got a chance to be in another *Star Wars* film because George [Lucas] had killed off his character."[43]

Replacing the Actors

The trend toward animating entire films employing CGI as well as using a mix of CGI and live performers is sure to continue as animation moves into the future. For example, in addition to the release of a new version of *The Lion King* in 2019, Disney also released new versions of two classic cel-animated features: *Dumbo* and *Aladdin*. Originally released in 1941, *Dumbo* tells the story of a baby elephant who uses his unusually large ears as wings—making him the hit of the circus. *Aladdin*, originally released in 1992, is an animated version of an old Arabian folktale about a young hero who finds a magic lamp containing a genie. The 2019 versions of both films feature a mix of live actors and CGI-created characters. In the new version of *Dumbo*, the elephant is animated; in *Aladdin*, the genie is a CGI version of actor Will Smith.

Animation industry insiders predict CGI will continue to dominate filmmaking into the future for the very simple reason that CGI helps studios make enormous profits. Audiences flock to such films—which is why Disney has made new versions of *The Lion King*, *Dumbo*, and *Aladdin* using CGI effects. Indeed, CGI-animated films such as *Frozen*, *Incredibles 2*, *Minions*, and *Toy*

Dumbo, released by Disney in 2019, features a mix of live actors and CGI characters. In this new version (pictured), the elephant is animated.

Story 3 have all garnered more than $1 billion in box office receipts.

Some observers believe that in the future, there will be no need for actors—that the entire production of what would otherwise have been a live-action film will be created by animators sitting at computer terminals. In other words, there will be no need to hire actors, camera operators, sound technicians, and the other professionals found on the typical movie set. To produce a sequel in the *Fast and the Furious* series, for example, there will be no need to film sleek cars racing along urban boulevards. Those scenes will, instead, be composed by animators sitting in their offices. Sfetcu says that "achieving such a goal would mean that conventional flesh-and-bone human actors are no longer necessary for this kind of movie creation, and computer animation would become the standard of making every kind of movie, not just animated movies."[44]

> "Flesh-and-bone human actors are no longer necessary for this kind of movie creation, and computer animation would become the standard of making every kind of movie, not just animated movies."[44]
>
> —Technology writer Nicolae Sfetcu

Other observers counter that audiences would not accept characters created entirely through CGI. They note that the talents of the actors and actresses in bringing their characters to life is what makes movies so popular. Technology writer Oon Yeoh agrees:

When that day comes will it make real life actors obsolete like cab drivers are expected to become obsolete once driverless cars become the norm? Probably not. A hyperrealistic CGI character that's not based on the image of a real life star might not have the same kind of appeal of say, a CGI character based on [action movie star] Bruce Lee. *Star Wars* fans were excited at the prospect of seeing Grand Moff Tarkin in *Rogue One* precisely because he's based on a real-life actor.

A CGI character that's completely made up and not based on the image of any famous actor will not have any star power. I think if a movie were to feature a CGI actor, it would be to resurrect a famous dead actor. . . . But a completely made-up CGI character not based on anyone famous? What's the point?[45]

Stories for Mature Audiences

Although the technology of animation has taken great leaps forward in recent years, especially in the areas of photorealism and CGI, the stories depicted through animation have not. After

"A CGI character that's completely made up and not based on the image of any famous actor will not have any star power."[45]

—Technology writer Oon Yeoh

all, for all the plaudits heaped on the CGI techniques employed in *The Lion King*, *Dumbo*, and *Aladdin*, the stories are still largely no different than their original versions. *Dumbo* recounts the adventures of a flying elephant. *Aladdin* tells the story of a magical genie who grants three wishes to the lovestruck hero. And *The Lion King* recounts the adventures of a lion cub who grows up to rule his fellow animals. Essentially, *The Lion King* is a talking animal story. None of these films present stories that truly reflect the challenges, pitfalls, and triumphs typically found in the lives of ordinary people.

BoJack Horseman is also a talking animal story—but it is much more. The TV series—produced through cel animation— can be found on the Netflix streaming service. The title character is a talking horse, but he is a talking horse with problems similar to those of many viewers.

BoJack is a washed-up actor who cannot find work in today's Hollywood. He is an alcoholic. He is depressed and has expressed suicidal thoughts. Although BoJack has largely himself to blame for his situation, he wallows in self-pity. Entertainment journalist Emily Nussbaum says, "He runs in circles. That's what addiction is, after all. BoJack's life is a formula, one that he feels desperate to correct: he's ashamed of who he is, attempts to become creative or feel love—and then inevitably binges, betrays a loved one, and runs away, realizing that it's impossible to truly repair the damage. Then back to shame."[46]

The Jetsons, the Flintstones, and even Homer and Marge Simpson never had to face such a terrible spiral of alcoholism, depression, and self-hate. "You're going to see even more [of

Some of the newer animated shows, such as BoJack Horseman, *feature traditional cel animation, but the themes and characters are far from traditional. In this TV series, the central character is a talking horse who is also a washed-up actor with a drinking problem.*

these types of stories] in the next five years, [including] a larger diversity of the kind of things we would call adult animation," says Raphael Bob-Waksberg who, along with Lisa Hanawalt, created and produces *BoJack Horseman*. He adds,

> There are networks that are interested in taking chances and reaching audiences on things [that] maybe they wouldn't before. I hope that leads to more opportunities for different types of people that earlier would not have been welcome in this industry or format. I am doing what I can to expand the tent and bring up other people and make sure we are telling different kinds of stories. I'm hopeful that trend continues.[47]

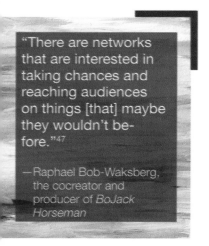

"There are networks that are interested in taking chances and reaching audiences on things [that] maybe they wouldn't before."[47]

—Raphael Bob-Waksberg, the cocreator and producer of *BoJack Horseman*

The Stories Grow Up

Since its debut in 2014, fans have embraced *BoJack Horseman*. In 2019 the website Internet Movie Database conducted a poll among fans to gauge the series' popularity. Fans were asked to rate the series on a scale of one to ten, with ten being the highest rating and one the lowest. Of the 67,505 viewers who responded, 56,371 gave the series a score of eight or better. Entertainment writer Carolyn Framke says,

> The reason *BoJack Horseman* is so good isn't just that it can knock the breath out of you with an expertly deployed gut punch; it's that it can do so seconds after knocking the breath out of you with an expertly deployed punchline. If one scene shows BoJack grappling with the darkest parts of his psyche, the next can include a TV news crawl delivering a killer joke like, "Giraffe CEO breaks glass ceiling."[48]

Disenchantment

Matt Groening created *The Simpsons* in 1989, establishing what has become the longest-running series—either animated or live action—in TV history. And while the show aims to amuse an adult audience, even Groening admits that the characters hardly reflect the traits and foibles of real people.

In 2018 Groening took his work in a new direction. He created the cel-animated show *Disenchantment*, which tells the story of three characters living in a mythical kingdom known as Dreamland. Although the story may be centered in a mythical land, audiences find the characters displaying very real emotions—including the main character, Princess Bean, a rebellious nineteen-year-old facing questions about the direction of her life. Netflix planned to stream the series at least through 2021.

According to *Disenchantment*'s executive producer, Josh Weinstein,

> It's a story of these three characters facing the world for the first time as an adult. All the adults and legends that come before tell you what you should do and how you should behave, but our characters are like, "No . . . we're going to find our own way." That's the underlying theme. You may not know what you're going to do in life, but with your friends, you'll find your way and yourself. We put a lot of our experiences of being that age and going into the world and not knowing what we want to do into this show. So in that way, it reflects the current world.

Quoted in Mike Bloom, "*Disenchantment* EP Josh Weinstein: Fantasy and Netflix Are a Magic Fit," *Hollywood Reporter*, August 17, 2018. www.hollywoodreporter.com.

The success of *BoJack Horseman* has promoted the development of other animated TV series written for adult audiences. Among the series that have been streamed on Netflix in recent years is *F Is for Family*. Set in the 1970s, *F Is for Family* tells the story of a dysfunctional family whose members find themselves dealing with such issues as losing their jobs, enduring bullies, failing at school, and rivalries among siblings. The show was created by comedian Bill Burr, who voices the character of loudmouth father Frank Murphy.

On the show, actor Justin Long voices the character of troubled teenage son Kevin. He says,

> Kevin has a deep voice and he's all testosterone. He's brimming with hormones. That's what's so fun about that character. There's a real freedom in just being constantly disgruntled by everything. Things happen to us in life and we're frustrated, but maybe it's just me, but that frustration has to go somewhere. Some people meditate, listen to music . . . however they allow that frustration to escape. The great thing about doing that show is, it's kind of therapeutic to play such a frustrated person. I get to yell at Bill Burr. There's no one more fun to yell at, because there's no one better at yelling and cursing than Bill Burr. It's like playing one-on-one basketball with LeBron [James]; you're doing it with the best. You're screaming at the best. It's really fun.[49]

F is for Family debuted in 2015; Netflix planned to stream episodes of the show at least through 2020.

As animation moves into the future, the day may arrive when fans are not sure whether what they are seeing on the screen was produced with actors or whether the characters were concocted completely on computer screens in a CGI animation studio. As for the stories fans are likely to see, they may find that as they have grown up, the scenarios unfolding in front of them have grown up as well.

ᏚOURCE NOTES

Introduction: Animation Transformation

1. Keith Scott, *The Moose That Roared: The Story of Jay Ward, Bill Scott, a Flying Squirrel, and a Talking Moose.* New York: St. Martin's Griffin, 2001, p. 106.
2. Joe Morgenstern, "Bart Simpson's Real Father: Recalling the Fear and Absurdity of Childhood, Matt Groening Has Created a Cartoon Sitcom More Human than Most Live-Action Shows," *Los Angeles Times*, April 29, 1990. www.latimes.com.

Chapter One: The History of Animation

3. Stephen Cavalier, *The World History of Animation*. Berkeley: University of California Press, 2011, p. 62.
4. J.P. Telotte, *Animating Space: From Mickey to WALL-E*. Lexington: University of Kentucky Press, 2010. Kindle.
5. Quoted in Neal Gabler, *Walt Disney: The Triumph of the American Imagination*. New York: Knopf, 2006, p. 127.
6. Quoted in Animation USA, "Warner Bros. Studio Biography." www.animationusa.com.
7. Quoted in Joe Tracy, "An Inside Look at the Original *Beauty and the Beast*," Digital Media FX, 2001. www.digitalmediafx.com.
8. Josh Larsen, "*Toy Story*," Larsen on Film. www.larsenonfilm.com.

Chapter Two: Artists of Influence

9. Quoted in Harry McCracken, "Luxo Sr.: An Interview with John Lasseter," *Harry-Go-Round* (blog). www.harrymccracken.com.
10. Quoted in Brent Schlender, "Pixar's Magic Man," *Fortune*, May 17, 2006. www.fortune.com.
11. Quoted in *Irish Examiner*, "Irish Woman Collaborated with Angelina Jolie on New Animated Film," November 9, 2017. www.irishexaminer.com.

12. Quoted in John Meagher, "From School Drop-Out to Oscar-Nominated Animator with Cartoon Saloon—Nora Twomey," *Sunday Independent* (Dublin, Ireland), June 11, 2017. www.independent.ie.
13. Quoted in Heather Mason, "An Interview with Nora Twomey, Director of *The Breadwinner*—a New Film That Tells the Amazing Story of an 11-Year-Old Afghan Girl," Amy Poehler's Smart Girls, December 1, 2017. www.amysmartgirls.com.
14. Quoted in Tatiana Hullender, "Miguel Jiron and David Schulenburg Interview: *Spider-Man: Into the Spider-Verse*," ScreenRant.com, February 25, 2019. https://screenrant.com.
15. Quoted in Ellen Wolff and Ramin Zahed, "*Animation Magazine*'s Rising Stars of 2018," *Animation Magazine*, March 30, 2018. www.animationmagazine.net.
16. Brian Lowry, "Oscars 2019: Who Will Win and Who Should in a Wide-Open Race," CNN.com, February 24, 2019. www.cnn.com.
17. A.O. Scott, "*Spider-Man: Into the Spider-Verse* Review: A Fresh Take on a Venerable Hero," *New York Times*, December 12, 2018. www.nytimes.com.
18. Quoted in Wolff and Zahed, "*Animation Magazine*'s Rising Stars of 2018."
19. Quote in Ko Ricker, "A Chat with *The Burden* Filmmaker Niki Lindroth von Bahr, Whose Films Will Be Screened in Montreal," Cartoonbrew, April 3, 2018. www.cartoonbrew.com.
20. Quoted in Lisa Gallagher, "TIFF 2017 Profile: Niki Lindroth von Bahr," *MUFF Blog*, Medium, September 10, 2017. https://medium.com.

Chapter Three: New Outlets for Animation

21. Quoted in Maureen Furniss, *A New History of Animation*. New York: Thames and Hudson, 2016, p. 320.
22. Alex Clark, "Extended Bio." www.itsalexclark.com.
23. Quoted in Tubefilter, "YouTube Millionaires: ItsAlexClark Finds It 'Really Fun to Figure Out How to Tell a Story,'" December 14, 2017. www.tubefilter.com.

24. Quoted in *Evening Standard* (London), "The Tom Ridgewell Show: The 22-Year-Old Making £10,000 a Month from His Bedroom on YouTube," March 12, 2013. www.standard.co.uk.
25. Quoted in Brent Lang, "Inside Netflix's Plans to Conquer Family Entertainment," *Variety*, November 6, 2018. https://variety.com.
26. Quoted in Lang, "Inside Netflix's Plans to Conquer Family Entertainment."
27. Jim Rutter, "Classic Hopeful Quest, Plus CGI," *Philadelphia Inquirer*, April 11, 2019, p. B7.
28. Peter Debruge, "Film Review: *Funan*," *Variety*, October 22, 2018. https://variety.com.

Chapter Four: The Changing Roles of Women in Animation

29. Quoted in Molly Lambert, "The Origin Story of the Depressingly Good 'BoJack Horseman,'" *New Yorker*, September 10, 2018. www.newyorker.com.
30. Quoted in Ramin Zahed, "*Tuca & Bertie*: Meet Lisa Hanawalt's Birds of a Feather," *Animation Magazine*, March 29, 2019. www.animationmagazine.net.
31. Quoted in Dana Schwartz, "Watch a First Look at Netflix's New Animated Series *Tuca & Bertie* Starring Tiffany Haddish and Ali Wong," *Entertainment Weekly*, March 14, 2019. https://ew.com.
32. Quote in Jenny Brewer, "Why Is There a Lack of Women in Animation, and What Can We Do About It?," It's Nice That, March 8, 2018. www.itsnicethat.com.
33. Quoted in Mary Beth Culler, "Look Closer: Women in the Disney Ink and Paint Department," *Walt Disney Family Museum Blog*, April 6, 2012. www.waltdisney.org.
34. Quoted in Skye Lobell, "Elizabeth Case Zwicker," Great Women Animators. http://greatwomenanimators.com.
35. Quoted in Terry Flores, "Women in Animation Leads Push to Get More Females into the Toon Business," *Variety*, February 4, 2016. https://variety.com.

36. Quoted in Wolff and Zahed, "*Animation Magazine*'s Rising Stars of 2018."

37. Adam Holmes, "Ghidorah Is Terrifying in New *Godzilla: King of the Monsters*," CinemaBlend, January 2019. www.cinema blend.com.

Chapter Five: The Future of Animation

38. Quoted in Oh My Disney, "King of the Jungle: The Making of *The Lion King*," 2016. https://ohmy.disney.com.

39. Janet Maslin, "The Hero Within the Child Within," *New York Times*, June 15, 1994, p. C-11.

40. Josh Weiss, "How Jon Favreau's *The Lion King* Will Justify Disney's Remake Frenzy," *Forbes*, February 25, 2019. www .forbes.com.

41. Nicolae Sfetcu, *The Art of Movies*. Bucharest, Romania: SetThings, 2011. Kindle.

42. Meghan Chou, "Uncanny Valley and the Future of Animation," March 21, 2018. *Michigan Daily* (University of Michigan, Ann Arbor), www.michigandaily.com.

43. Quoted in Andrew Pulver, "*Rogue One* VFX Head: 'We Didn't Do Anything Peter Cushing Would've Objected To,'" *Guardian* (Manchester, UK), January 16, 2017. www.theguardian.com.

44. Sfetcu, *The Art of Movies*.

45. Oon Yeoh, "Is CGI the Future of Acting?" *New Straits Times* (Malaysia), December 2, 2018. www.nst.com.my.

46. Emily Nussbaum, "The Bleakness and Joy of 'BoJack Horseman,'" *New Yorker*, August 1, 2016. www.newyorker.com.

47. Quoted in Mike Bloom, "From *BoJack Horseman* to *Rick and Morty*: Inside the Rise of Animated Comedy," *Hollywood Reporter*, September 14, 2018. www.hollywoodreporter.com.

48. Caroline Framke, "*BoJack Horseman* Is Famous for Being Emotionally Wrenching. But It's Also Ridiculously Funny," Vox, September 21, 2017. www.vox.com.

49. Quoted in Zak Wojnar, "Justin Long Interview: Tall Tales," Screen Rant, January 9, 2019. https://screenrant.com.

$\mathscr{F}$OR FURTHER RESEARCH

Books

Maureen Furniss, *A New History of Animation*. New York: Thames & Hudson, 2016.

Mindy Johnson, *Ink & Paint: The Women of Walt Disney's Animation*. Glendale, CA: Disney Editions, 2017.

Jasmine Katatikarn and Michael Tanzillo, *Lighting for Animation: The Art of Visual Storytelling*. Boca Raton, FL: CRC, 2017.

Mike Reiss and Mathew Klickstein, *Springfield Confidential: Jokes, Secrets, and Outright Lies from a Lifetime Writing for "The Simpsons."* New York: HarperCollins, 2018.

Susannah Shaw, *Stop Motion: Craft Skills for Model Animation*. Boca Raton, FL: CRC, 2017.

Internet Sources

Terry Flores, "Women in Animation Leads Push to Get More Females into the Toon Business," *Variety*, February 4, 2016. https://variety.com.

Brent Lang, "Inside Netflix's Plans to Conquer Family Entertainment," *Variety*, November 6, 2018. https://variety.com.

John Meagher, "From School Drop-Out to Oscar-Nominated Animator with Cartoon Saloon—Nora Twomey," *Sunday Independent* (Dublin, Ireland), June 11, 2017. www.independent.ie.

Emily Nussbaum, "The Bleakness and Joy of 'BoJack Horseman,'" *New Yorker*, August 1, 2016. www.newyorker.com.

Ellen Wolff and Ramin Zahed, "*Animation Magazine*'s Rising Stars of 2018," *Animation Magazine*, March 30, 2018. www.animation magazine.net.

Websites

Animation Magazine (animationmagazine.net). The online version of the animation industry's main trade journal provides news of developments in animation, a guide to animated feature films planned for future release, and a list of American and international universities where students can major in animation.

Annecy Festival (www.annecy.org). Maintained by the Annecy International Animation Film Festival, this website provides updates on the nominees vying for the animation industry's top award. By accessing the link for "Volunteers, Interns and Jobs," young people can learn about the opportunities to work at the annual festival held in Annecy, France, near Geneva, Switzerland.

CalArts Character Animation (https://filmvideo.calarts.edu/programs/character-animation). Maintained by the animation department at the California Institute of the Arts, this website explains the program of studies for potential students who are considering animation as a major. The website includes films produced by CalArts students as well as images of individual cels composed by students.

Ray and Diana Harryhausen Foundation (www.rayharryhausen.com). The foundation works to preserve the models crafted by stop-motion pioneer Ray Harryhausen. Visitors to the foundation's website can find photos of Harryhausen at work, crafting assorted miniature monsters, lizards, and other beasts; a list of museums that feature exhibits of Harryhausen's models; and podcasts recorded by experts discussing Harryhausen's work.

Women in Animation (https://womeninanimation.org). Established in 1995, WIA helps women find careers in animation. Although some of the website content is limited to WIA members, visitors can access stories reporting on the accomplishments of female animators, a schedule of workshops for prospective animators, and videos of seminars that help women establish themselves in the profession.

INDEX

PICTURE CREDITS

Cover: Nearbirds/Depositphotos

9: Fox Network/Photofest

11: Photofest

14: Warner Bros. Pictures/Album/Newscom

20: Disney/Photofest

23: Pixar Animation Studios/Walt Disney Pictures/Album/
Newscom

27: Universal Studios/Photofest

30: Columbia Pictures Corp/Lord Miller/Pascal Pic/SPE/
Marvel/Album/Newscom

35: Kyodo/AP Images

40: Fabian Sommer/dpa/picture-alliance/Newscom

43: Norbert Falco/ZUMApress/Newscom

45: Stephen Smith/Sipa USA/Newscom

50: Fox Broadcasting/Photofest

52: Netflix/Photofest

56: Walt Disney Pictures/Photofest

60: Walt Disney Studios Motion Pictures/Photofest

63: Netflix/Album/Newscom

Craig E. Blohm has written numerous books and magazine articles for young readers. He and his wife, Desiree, reside in Tinley Park, Illinois.

Hal Marcovitz is a former newspaper reporter and columnist. He has written nearly two hundred books for young readers. His other books in the Art Scene series are *The Art of Graffiti* and *The Art of Tattoos*. He makes his home in Chalfont, Pennsylvania.